Habitation
Of Wonder

The Poiema Poetry Series

Poems are windows into worlds; windows into beauty, goodness, and truth; windows into understandings that won't twist themselves into tidy dogmatic statements; windows into experiences. We can do more than merely peer into such windows; with a little effort we can fling open the casements, and leap over the sills into the heart of these worlds. We are also led into familiar places of hurt, confusion, and disappointment, but we arrive in the poet's company. Poetry is a partnership between poet and reader, seeking together to gain something of value—to get at something important.

Ephesians 2:10 says, "We are God's workmanship . . ." *poiema* in Greek— the thing that has been made, the masterpiece, the poem. The Poiema Poetry Series presents the work of gifted poets who take Christian faith seriously, and demonstrate in whose image we have been made through their creativity and craftsmanship.

These poets are recent participants in the ancient tradition of David, Asaph, Isaiah, and John the Revelator. The thread can be followed through the centuries—through the diverse poetic visions of Dante, Bernard of Clairvaux, Donne, Herbert, Milton, Hopkins, Eliot, R. S. Thomas, and Denise Levertov—down to the poet whose work is in your hand. With the selection of this volume you are entering this enduring tradition, and as a reader contributing to it.

—D.S. Martin
Series Editor

Habitation
Of Wonder

ABIGAIL CARROLL

CASCADE *Books* · Eugene, Oregon

HABITATION OF WONDER

The Poiema Poetry Series

Cascade Books
An Imprint of Wipf and Stock Publishers
199 W. 8th Ave., Suite 3
Eugene, OR 97401

www.wipfandstock.com

PAPERBACK ISBN: 978-1-5326-3025-5
HARDCOVER ISBN: 978-1-5326-3027-9
EBOOK ISBN: 978-1-5326-3026-2

Cataloguing-in-Publication data:

Names: Carroll, Abigail
Title: Habitation of wonder / Abigail Carroll.
Description: Eugene, OR: Cascade Books, 2018 | Series: The Poiema Poetry Series.
Identifiers: ISBN 978-1-5326-3025-5 (paperback) | ISBN 978-1-5326-3027-9 (hardcover) | ISBN 978-1-5326-3026-2 (ebook)
Subjects: LCSH: subject | subject | subject | subject
Classification: CALL NUMBER 2018 (paperback) | CALL NUMBER (ebook)

Manufactured in the U.S.A.   12/22/17

To my parents, who taught me wonder.

Contents

AIR

WORD

CREED

Genesis (I)

We read the Word
spoke forth creation, but
I'm not so sure it wasn't
sung into being,

not exactly hummed,
though insects might
have appeared with hardly
an opening of the mouth.

No doubt, the sun
was spun from delicate,
yet forceful arias—thus
the operatic nature of light.

Out of a bass-line, deep
blue tones—the kind you
rarely hear until they've
faded into air—whales.

Ostriches sprang from
strange improvisations.
Elephants are echoes
of ancient, sacred chants.

I imagine larkspur, phlox,
and clover are the progeny
of nursery rhymes repeated
quaintly, readily, musingly,

as if sheer gratuity
were their purpose, as if
they were made for nothing
more than loveliness. Stars,

in their totality, emerged
not from a tune, but rather
a soft and knowing sound:
a buzz, a kind of celestial

purr, a note so perfectly
content with itself that
it sparked, became what
it dreamed: a universe.

WATER

Canticle (I)

To agree with the lake.
To sing and let sing
bristle grass, a white sail,
beach stones
mottling the shore
in music older
than the human ear.
To be tutored
by a bent reed,
the smooth back
of driftwood
listing, concurring.
To let nouns be nouns
the way the mountains
inhabit the grammar
of their waiting,
the way hawks
refuse to apologize
for flight.
To let in the light
like earth lets in
the shining prophecies
of rain,
like monarchs
let summer dance
gold on the open invitation
of their wings.
To brother the wind.
Not to choose between
tomorrow and today.

Not to refuse the liturgies
of the waves,
the rhetoric
of the glittering sun
spilt.
To be undone.
To note the descant
of a cloud, a cormorant,
tree crickets' hum,
the signature
of glaciers scrawled
on lichen rock.
To defer to the willow.
Not to prefer ignorance
to the theories of swallows,
the languages of the air.
To enter the concert,
the stirring,
the singing,
the way the bulrush enters
its blooming,
the way sky enters
the glow of evening,
the green-turning-flame
of its song.

The Calling

And so it is, the lake is calling you,
      dropping in your ear the small consonants

of its lapping. There is no resisting.
      It insists on shivering water into light.

You have beheld this silver before.
      In dreams, it's the radiance you wear.

The jangle of shroud against mast:
      a language you have come to understand.

It has let you in on its secret. So too
      has the dark slipping by of the cormorant.

Soft, the verbiage of a passing
      kayak, the lisp of the paddle's dip and rise,

the narrow body's thin blue glide.
      A word has perched on your tongue, but

refuses to be formed, tastes like
      storm-rinsed sky, the wind-downed

rhetoric of pines imitating the slow dance
      of waves. Acquainted with all manner of

waiting, the dock grows patient
      with your sitting, your staring, your curious

forward-leaning. Listen: water
     tapping, pulling at the hull, the metal siding

on the plank-wood pier. It circles out
     from your dangling ankles, a shimmering

map of echoes, farther, farther—one
     rippled articulation after another. The lake

is a mirror, a question you cannot answer—
     yet one you choose to enter.

Make Me River

Make me river, cold
with mountain, green
with quiver, silver in

the run and churn of
winter leaving, valley
waking, sheet moss

breathing. Make me
flash of mica, drift of
foam. O Lord of flux,

make these dry bones
flow, teach me to spill,
pool, glide, fall, tutor me

to long for depth, seek
downward paths, indwell
the low. Oh teach me

liturgy of keel, swirl,
flume, the breaking into
mist, the pull, the press,

the song. Oh form me
into blood of bedrock,
quest of glacier, dream

of sea, release me, set
me free to course, surge,
pour, sweep, issue, eddy,

shower, plummet, roll.
O Lord of flood, O Lord
of spray, unstill my soul.

The Way A Fish

The way a fish
  moves through water,
    through light, the way light
doubles the body
  of the fish, turns it
    into a mirror of itself,
the mirror being
  the water's invitation
    to see a bright pool
of scales where
  once there was a fish,
    a school of silver coins,
a great, green-glass
  chandelier dangling
    in the flow, each cut-glass
drop sewn like sequins
  to the wind, the wind being
    the way the water moves
around the coins,
  the coins being another
    way to see the fish, the way
it moves through
  water, through light
    the way it doubles, becomes
a silver mirror, the mirror
  being the fish disappearing
    into a thousand versions of itself.

Learning To Pray

When I say I have passed the afternoon
watching loosestrife lean against the wind
at the edge of the lake, what I mean is

I have stepped into prayer, not unlike Peter
stepping out of the boat, and it has held me,
as prayer does, like a child holds a penny,

or ferns hold beads of dew. When slippage
occurs, as it is want to do, and I begin to sink
through unraveling molecules of faith like

a dream sinks back into dark when dawn
dissolves the net of sleep, I am caught by a
quiet grip, an open palm, the way air catches

a parachute or a June buttercup catches light,
and there is in that catching a new kind of
drowning, not unpleasant, though it surprises

at first. It's like losing yourself to an embrace
in which the more you are lost, the more
surely you are found; it's like the flood of sun

on the map of your skin, into your cells
and the spaces between your cells, sewing
you into its warmth, which, you realize,

is singing. How often have I stood at the edge
of the lake gazing, wholly unsure what it means
to pray but willing to step out, willing to go

down, slip through the watery blue particles
precisely to be caught, recovered, salvaged
again and again, to know once more that hand!

Make Me Chalice

Make me chalice, bowl of tears
and wine. Mold me valley deep.
Make curve this earth you wedge,
pinch, lute, glaze, coil, shape.

Oh make me open palm, vessel
of praise and doubt, basin of
dusk. Carve wide the lip, form
broad the hull, O Lord of clay.

Make room for rain; make room
for song. And I will be the moon,
which holds the sun and pours it
forth. And I will be the well that

Jacob built. Oh hollow me. Oh
make me yours to fill, to lift,
to bless, to spill. And I will be de-
canted. Yes, and I will be refilled.

Thalassic

Haunt of salp
and red-shelled crab—here lives
            the mouthless, sac-bodied

tubeworm:
white finger tentacled to vents
            and cold seeps, feeding

on water
and sulfur and dark. Kingdom
            of the lungless,

the gill-raked,
the swim-bladdered: the eel-like
            hagfish,

scavenger
of whale falls; the "snot-flower" bone-eater,
            feather-plumed

burrower.
Behold: the gulper, the swallower, all manner
            of loosejaw,

the wide-gaped,
blunt-snouted citizens of the deep—
            dragon-faced

fangtooths
hanging in the blackness, hinge-skulled
            viperfish

barbel-luring
hermit crabs. Consider also the bulb-eyed
            jewel squid,

hovering
umbrella under-studded with stars,
            and the silver-

scaled eye-ring
of the star-washed lanternfish, thin-finned,
            dazzle-tailed firefly

of the brine.
This is the province of the spike-eyed
            and light-averse,

canyon-dwellers,
night-dwellers, breathers of cold and salt.
            This is the empire

of the armor-shelled
and carapaced, the saw-tooth clawed,
            the tendril-danglers,

the glowers, the snappers,
            the mute.

M Is for Mary

Hampton Bays, Long Island

M is for Mary, Mother of God,
        patron saint of suburban front lawns,
                blue-mantled friend of sinners and pinwheels,

mollusk-studded mailboxes,
        moss-dotted patios. M is for Medjugorje,
                Massapequa, moon jellies washed up

like useless musings on the shore,
        a menagerie of bathers: misguided,
                metallic in their shine. Gulls beak marram grass,

mica flakes,
        mussel shells, empty packs
                of Marlboros. M is for the millions—

the reverent, the mystified—
        Moxie drinkers, marina workers,
                mahjongg-players, Matlock watchers—

the Madjeskas, yellow lanterns
        garlanding their porch, Manilow
                on the radio, macramé scratching the backs

of our legs. Cardinals mount
        the arch of the holy white
                plaster, hop between birdbath and mulberry,

consider the minor miracle
        of perpetual posture. Our Lady of
                Bay Avenue, of marigolds, milk cans, mayweed,

Madonna of the mullet-anglers,
        mooring-fixers, lemon meringue makers:
                you preside over mainsail and mizzen mast,

the maintenance of motors,
        the scrubbing of mildewed hulls, the spreading
                of garden mulch. M is for the fog horn's distant,

plaintive moan, for plastic mass cards
        on the fridge, Montauk daisies in the breeze,
                mackerel frying on the stove.

Heron

Across the water
from the shipyard—
lights glittering
over the bodies
of nuclear submarines—
and not far
from the fishing pier
where the *Lost Cause*,
the *Elizabeth-Kate*,
and the *Special K*
are moored, you stand,
thin as a prospect, so still
I take you first for a sculptor's
joke, your stoic beak forged
toward the distant hum
and bang
of industry.
We study the gray
feathered stick of you,
at first unfindable
with binoculars
some strangers lend us,
then unsteady in the lens.
My fingers brush the cold,
paint-chipped rail;
I wrap and unwrap
my ankle around the pole,
waiting for you to move,
waiting for the couple

with the binoculars
to stop watching,
wondering if you are
for real, and what *is* real
about the evening—
the glistening shipyard sparks
exploding in the distance,
the reeking nets, lobster traps
stacked high on the docks,
a rusted red truck perched
at the end of the pier,
and here, where the water
laps a tiny
pebble-gray shore,
your perfect plumage,
the bold show of it,
your awkward audience,
unsure how long to stand,
whether or not to wait for a sign
to break the calm and head back
toward the car, away
from the gleaming pink face
of the sky.

Vespers

Incense and stone: the mountains
        rehearse their certitudes, enter

the ancient contours of their vigils,
        holding up what remains of the day's

undoing. These are the offices of the evening.
        I sit at the grassy edge and watch a cormorant's

low descent, the black sentence of her wings
        skirting the water's quiet lip. The sky is a prayer

repeating across the lake in cindered grays—
        a dash between the fragile lease on light,

the question marks that constitute
        the dark. A graphite scrawl of dusk retreats

to where the mallards look, slips past the rim
        to where the tenses sleep. The pause begins:

cold stars appear; they spell night's contract
        with the air, spit and blink their little codes.

Who knows what secret vowels are theirs
        and what the splintered moon implies?

White comma in the breath of space,
        mute trace of lost vernaculars.

WOOD(S)

May

Rachael Carson National Wildlife Refuge, Wells, Maine

Odd-angled branches
    point outward—some skyward—
        from the crooked cylinders

of the pines,
    each arm the frozen gesture
        of a winter; together, a broken ladder.

The yellow-turning-green
    of the underbrush is its own story.
        Leaves unfold from the tips of saplings

like small maps of summer;
    already, they have forgotten
        the tight round architecture of the bud.

The trees have carved
    shifting columns of light from the self-gift
        of the sun. Black flies suspend themselves

like afterthoughts
    in the shining, perforate the humid air.
        I am taken by the curled green tongue

of a fern, turned
    inward, yet reaching thinly upward,
        delicate as the dangling green filaments

of hickories in spring,
       or the seven white points of a starflower.
              A swallow darts sharply. Another follows.

Crows announce
       their place in the kingdom
              of odd-angled branches; on their perches,

finches preen, bob
       their little yellow heads. Blue jays
              congratulate the sky.

Habitation of Wonder

And the granite was ours, its
rippled grain cool under our
hands, and the granite was
a home, a compass to a home,
the habitation of our wonder,
and the squirrels looked down
from the rough pines. Ours
was the birch and the maple—
the leaves and the interstices
between the leaves. Through
them peered a blue so calm,
so water-like it might have
been left over from the birth
of the world. And the wind
went about its languages
above us, and the wind held
our secrets in its giant open
ear. Ours were arrangements
of lichen, moss, stone. We read
them like Braille, our fingers
light and needing the edges
of things. And the damp bled
through our coats, and the damp
was toadstools and ink caps
asserting their theories of time.
Ours was time. We stayed
till a distant windowed glow
pierced the scrim of dusk.

And the rock sang us its shadow,
and the rock was our domesticity,
and the rock was all we knew.

for Cozette

Make Me Sheet Moss

Make me sheet moss,
attender to shagbark,
leaf song, liverwort, dew,
the muculent lives of snails,
the wine of fungi, wood rot,
humus, duff. School me to
love mineral, lichen frond,
sphagnum, cort, subsist on
mist, on drip of sky, on evening
damp. Tutor me to comfort
stone, and I will soothe the
ground, yes I will bless the
clod, bandage stump and limb
and twig, companion crags,
mend ruptured seams in trunks—
in cedar, alder, balsam, oak—
and I will heal the ancient
wounds of ice-scarred rock,
salve the grief of upturned
earth, yes I will learn to prize
the meek, the gradual,
the diminutive, the low—
O Lord of root,
of mica,
of loam.

Maine

Cloaked in the cry of a loon across the milk-moon
lake, the distinct risk of a call—the summons

of a sky that spells *north* in an atlas of stars. Ferns
lisp, balsams lean. I listen for the small movements

of deer, their route forged by an underground compass
of salt. At stake in the boreal passages of night geese

and the small certitudes of waves against a plank-
and-frame skiff: the unseen claim of a cardinal point—

and with that claim, the very notion of plot (primeval
tilt, perpetual cant). Moth wings flick the cabin screen.

Wool-damp against my skin, I lay caught between
twin imperatives: travel and sleep, each a map

to that kingdom whose edge is the far shore of the lake,
that country whose gate is the pine-branched dark.

That I Might Dwell

That I might dwell in warbler
song, in fields of sorrel, fields
of stars, that dwelling in your
house I'd know, I'd rest, I'd play
at wonder. Oh that I might dwell

in pine-branched shade, among
the sway, among the praise of oak-
fern, granite, jay nest, spruce—
among the shadow-dance of leaves,
the breeze unpinning doubt, all

apathy, all hollow hours, all fears.
Oh may I dwell in reverence here,
and dwelling in your house, I'll
wait, I'll pray, I'll lay this body
down on what you've dreamed,

on what you've sung, spliced, spun,
twined, embroidered, breathed.
And dwelling in your house I'll
know the peace of moss, the moth-
winged hush of unhinged awe,

musk of sage, gaze of deer. Oh let
me lose myself in rooms of fox-
glove, cowslip, wild plum, wren—
that I might taste the sleep of loam,
that I might tenant beauty here.

Hallowed Be

O Father, who art in heaven,
        I saw your name:

It was tall as the oak
        I grew up under,

the bark grooves deep enough
        to tuck my fingers into.

Hallowed was the vine
        circling up the trunk,

the small leaves of it shivered
        the way beauty

shivers on the tongue.
        Your kingdom come

was a stone skimmed
        into the deep pocket

of the sea, waiting
        to be retrieved—I loved

the small impossibility
        of it. *Trespasses,*

I was pretty sure,
        resembled postage stamps,

orderly and official.
        I imagined my collection

would one day be impressive.
        Looming storm clouds

were *the power and the glory*:
        the kind you feel

before you see, the kind
        that carve a hollow

in your throat, that make
        the dark sky holy.

Concession

The beech is on loan
to the wind. Look:
a convoy of missives.
What is a leaf
but a letter—a tree's
summertime memo
to winter? Surrender:
it's what the kale stalks
refuse, the globe thistles
spurn. But consider
the long-kept secret of red—
glory. Behold the creed
of maples, the high
offices of hawthorn
and sumac. A skein
of fire is the chokeberry
by the pond, burning
briar—sun snagged
in the act of exit, tricked
into a dazzling, brief tango
with the branches—something
about a ransom. The phlox
by the fence have submitted
their resignation; the bare sticks
of the lilies, artifacts
of yielding. Gone the bees;
rusted, the asters. Cattails
relinquish their down.

Make Me Willow

Make me willow, pillar
of lament. Teach me to
bend. Send your breath,
gale that arcs the birch,
pries the pod, soars the
wing. Undo my vow to
lineal things—the tall,
the straight, the proud,
all that stands erect, all
that falls. Oh tutor me
in tears if tears need be.
Oh teach me to bow, to
lean, to verge, to yield.
Instruct my fisted hands
to cede. Apprentice my
knees. Let sing the gust.
Let rain release itself in
me. What good the sky?
What good the stars? Oh
school my hair to brush
the earth, my forehead
friend the dust. Oh let
this rigid will of steel
give way. Remake me.
Teach me how to sway.

The Glassed World

Wood tearing interrupted
 the night, branches ripping
through branches, the splitting
 of a trunk, its loud split-

second cleaving,
 the rough, splintered
dividing of its strong
 body. Then, the echoing:

ice falling on ice;
 glass sheets slipping
off the needles, wind-
 loosened from the branches—

a tempest of shattering,
 an orchestra of crashing.
In the morning was the blinding:
 the dazzling white arches

of the birches; the sharp,
 sun-white blades
of their broken switches; slick,
 glaring casements windowing

red berries; the thorns and torn
 stalks, stuck in their vestments.
Then, the melting, the inevitable
 unsheathing—the slow

drop-letting of what the trees
   carried, what their bent
branches bore; the streaming of it
   down the knotted bark of their dark

trunks, across the thawing moss,
   the still-green grass, into ponds
and gutter-pools, rock-lined
   streams, into the small river

of the ice-glistening street.
   At dusk, the dampness hardened;
night stopped the singing, stopped
   the moving water in the very shape

of its flowing. Now, the white face
   of the moon is rising, glaring
at the wind-riddled trees. Ice-laced,
   illuminated, they stare back, rattling.

Make Me Cello

Make me cello, tree of string
and drone. Teach me to hold
song, to groan, turn friction
into praise, sustain a note in

time. Oh render me unmute,
and I will learn to pray, forge
voice from wood and bow,
fiber of hair. Yes, and I will

timbre the air with hymn and
litany and lilt, with Hannah's
sighs, with David's lament. Oh
tune me, tutor me in sorrow

and desire. Oh sound me deep
as thunder roll, as bed of sea.
O Lord of scale and fugue—
compose your splendor on me.

March, Vermont

Annual wreckage laid bare
    by retreating snow:
shagbark littering the yard,
    black-spotted nut husks

the squirrels are long done
    with, a child's plastic
racecar, its dented wheels stuck,
    windshield crushed,

the thin-stemmed remains
    of last fall's phlox,
bleached and stained, flat
    as regret; shards

of slate the walkway discarded,
    granite and mica
the garden coughed up, faded
    receipt for lozenges,

a maple limb dis-armed:
    casualty of wind
and snow-turned-rain-turned-ice;
    an overabundance

of salt. Green has not yet
    occurred to the ground—
open wound dank with leaf-mold
    and under-earth—

nor to the crooked, bud-less oak,
    frozen in its rigorous
winter gesture. Phoebes
    cannot heal

this landscape of refusals, insist
    tritely as they do;
grackles scar the yard en masse,
    then move on

to the scar the next. Rakes
    and trowels,
glossed envelopes of seeds:
    all toys to distract

the heart, which, injured
    by the too-long cold,
the stifling dearth of verdance,
    must never catalogue

its damages, nor
    attempt to settle accounts
with the cold—waster,
    scavenger, thief.

Matins

Then will I weave,
from the ash-blue light
  and the laments

of David, a basket—
the spokes of which will hold,
  strong and bone-like,

a weft of words
soaked in solitude and moon-
  gleam, supple

as the waning dark,
which bends away on the arc
  of night. Then

will I twine
my petitions onto the dawn
  with each tuck

and fold, *Selah*.
Such is the work of prayer:
  a thrush sews twigs

and grass, and out
of it the bowl of a nest;
  chafed hands

braid reeds
and splints into a tabernacle
    of sorts. Here

    will I live—
if You will tenant this house:
    scaffold of birdsong,

    sighs, the grievances
of Job, stir of leaves, thread
    of light, breath of oaks.

AIR

Flyers and Singers

Anthems
of insects insist
on the end
of August. Thick
breathes the morning
with the promise
of finches—
short-winged,
orange-beaked
messengers
of the sun;
round-breasted, perched
orchestrations
of light.
I ankle
through ferns;
dew and jewel-
weed anoint
my pant-legs. Here
is the opening
in the woods
by the river;
here, the province
of flyers and singers,
who prophesy
in whistles
and quavers
and swoops. Clothed
in foliage,
they conspire

with the oak, dwell
in that fragile bright
shiver of green.
Theirs is the language
of height,
the lost continent
of wind; theirs
the secret sky-paths
of seeds. Me,
I come from the kingdom
of loam; my bones
are made of mud
and stone—of mud
and stone and a pocket
of breath. I fill my lungs
with the bird-throated air,
the river-washed air, air
mapped by bees
stealing blaze
from the phlox,
air sewn through
by a sparrow's
lightning dart.
Listen: the damp earth
respires. A flash
of yellow startles
the water. This place
is all wings and tongues
and fire.

Kingdom of the Air

Shifting bands of gawking geese
echo through the wood smoke air—
strangers in this time and place,
strange and wonderful as time

which also echoes through gray air,
realm of beaks and hollow bones,
wonderful and strange as light,
turning, shifting, as tricks unfold

the realm of beaks and hollow bones.
The vast blue desert of the sky—
it turns and shifts, plays tricks, beholds
a circling hawk that makes his home

the vast blue desert of the wind.
There are no lines or angles here;
the hawk that makes his home the air
invents his path with dawn-like wings.

Here there are no angles, lines,
only changing shapes of clouds,
paths carved out by dawn-like wings,
unmapped breath above the ground.

Make Me Red–tailed Hawk

Make me red-tailed hawk,
prince of feather and wing
and flight. O Lord of height,
shape me to glide the roof
of the storm, pilot the crease
of the wind. Oh let me see for
once the smallness of things,
the thinness of line between
city and field, between salt-
marsh and bay, between beauty
and grief. Teach me to mount,
to soar, to rise above the curse
of gravity, of stone. O Lord
of whirlwind, make me hollow-
boned, swift and light, twin of
eagle, twin of owl, twin of sky.
Yes, and I will skirr the breeze;
yes, and I will dance the air. Oh
and fields will go on blooming,
bowing, cities pushing, crowd-
ing, plowing, but I will drift,
and drifting, sing. Yes, I will
rise above the little things.

In Gratitude (I)

For *h,* tiny fire
    in the hollow of the throat,
        opener of every *hey,*

hi, how are you?,
    hello; chums with *c,*
        with *t,* shy lover of s;

there and not
    there—never seen,
        hardly heard, yet

real as air
    fluttering the oak,
        holding up the hawk;

the sound
    of a yawn, of sleep, of heat,
        a match, its quivering

orange flame
    turning wood into light,
        light into breath;

the sound
    of stars if stars
        could be heard, perhaps

the sound
    of space; life speaking life:
        warm air endowed

to hard clay—
    a heart, hurt,
        a desire to be healed—

the work
    of bees stuck in the nubs
        of hollyhocks

and columbine, time
    to the extent that time
        is light, is bright

as the match,
    the flame of the sun,
        real as the muffled hush

of sleep,
    the fluttering oak,
        a moth, the silent *oh*

in the throat
    when a hand is laid
        upon the shoulder;

hunger—
    the body's empty cry
        for filling, for loving,

for knowing
    the intimacy of breath,
        of half-breathed words

fragile as the stars:
    hollow, hush,
        holy.

Genesis (II)

First, blue,
> the feathered back of a heron,
> the dark underbelly of a wave;
an idea made visible:
> a breath, the way breath
>> is both sound and air,
> body and word.

Then, delight,
> the timeless gaze
> of a lover of art, the wild dart
>> of two sparrows in a dance
>> above the pines.
A perfectly gratuitous confusion: glory
> turning itself into glory.

Then, love,
> an explosion,
> the fallout of which we are, and are
> surrounded by: a deep, spinning, galactic
>> multiplicity of blue.
> Particles of breath in search
> of words, we are prone
to tinkering with sea glass, apt
> to wonder at the sky.

Enterprise

I do not pretend to understand
the enterprise
      of a field, the sibilating
      industry
of its grasses,
      seed pods
      conducting elaborate explosions
of white, the holy
      productivity of petal, nectar,
            bee.

I do not allege to apprehend
the vocation
      of the wind, its private,
      whispered
appointments
      with lupine,
      monarch wing, sky—its contracts
with stratus, with
      cumulous, with hurricane, with
            leaf.

I do not profess to comprehend
the devotion
      of a worm, its dark, ritual
      tunneling,
its precision
      engineering of
      leaf rot into loam, mute architect
of soil, proprietor
      of fungi, feldspar, cellulose,
          seed.

Cumulus

Blush-colored declaratives
of restlessness
and grace.
Balletic certitudes
edging
the known world.
Gestures
of light, suspensions
of dew
appareling
the going under
of day
in self-contained
prophecies of salmon
and ash.
Lambent pink nests
of fog,
brash, colossal pockets
of dream,
unhurried solitudes of rose
and dusk
and tulle
well practiced in the art
of likeness,
adagio,
motif.
Robed philosophes

deliberating the breath-pale
suggestion
of the
ascending moon,
concurring
with the pronounced
directionality
of the
wind.

A Short History of Light

I.
Out of a word, the sun.
Light incising water,
conspiring with matter.

Fire: a single orange
flint-breathed spark, its oily
gleam on ash-streaked skin.

The searing of carcasses,
stone-circle blazes, tomb-
illuminated solstices.

II.
A lamp: the grease-filled
hollow of a rock, a fish
threaded to a wick.

Torches: kindled
smoking bouquets of sticks.
Burnished marble dials turn

the sun into time. Per Plato:
light radiates from the eyes—
an entrapment of fireflies.

III.
String dipped in tallow.
Behold: the candle. Glass
reinvents itself as window,

gives birth to the spectacle.
The mirror: first copper,
then mica, then silver. In

stone-floored banquet halls,
candelabra: suspended
constructs of glimmer.

IV.
Enter gas, the match,
the Argand lamp: its vitreous
chimney, its hollow wick.

Soon in a lab: a filament,
a charge, a fist-sized globe
of glass. The dance of

incandescence. Second
Genesis. Miniature
ignition of a universe.

V.
Floodlights, spotlights,
marquises; expanding
constellation of screens.

Above: the city's footprint
on the sky—starless, ghost-
gowned sea. Inside: advance

from the sun—the white
spiraled coil of bottled fire
by which I write, you read.

Ode to Onions

Blue-glazed pot
bunched with onions.
Early August,
heat hanging
in every room,
the veined globes
bare white;
their pungent milk
flows
through the afternoon.
Theirs is the kitchen,
the counter—
they reign
over cookbooks,
the cutting board,
the blue-bottled windowsill,
glow like a bowl
of twilight moons.
Soon,
these moons will be halved,
knife-splayed,
each perfect ring
betrayed
by the quick silver's
downward dash;
a mist
thick with pepper
and summer
rises over the

backcountry, its hammocks
and insects, its silk-
tasseled cornfields.
Oil will impregnate the onion—
garlic, zucchini
conspire with it;
tomatoes will spill
their watery rhetoric.
Salt adds evidence
of the ocean, each grain
a curio
of the beach,
the burn of the sun.
A carnival
has arrived:
colored lights,
the sizzle of grease,
a Ferris wheel of flavors.
The onion
is the pop
of balloons
at the point of a dart,
the splash
of the dunking booth,
the sausage man's sweat,
the palm-reader's breath,
her azure eyes thick
with silver.
The ivory bulb offers itself
to the tongue,
the muffled sting
of its white-fire flesh;
it is the swoosh of air
through the metal grate
in the highest gondola,
the crack and shimmer
of sparklers short-circuiting

the night, lighting up
the wide eyes of children,
each bite
an awakening.

Swinging

Grown-up people are not strong enough to exult in monotony.

G.K. Chesterton

To move, to fly,
　　to travel the air on the seat
　　　　of a swing, bend your knees and lean
　　　　　　into the bend, extend the pendulum

of your legs
　　toward the jagged green points
　　　　of the pines, tap the blue rim
　　　　　　of the sky with the scuffed rubber soles

of your shoes,
　　fall back into the pillow
　　　　of the wind like into the welcome voice
　　　　　　of a friend; to fall hopelessly in love

with the air,
　　offer it your hair, the flailing hems
　　　　of your corduroy pants, the rasping flap
　　　　　　of your hood against your back

like the wing
　　of a tireless bird; to watch
　　　　the ground depart and return,
　　　　　　then depart again, to swoop

as if each dip
    and height were rehearsals for the next,
        as if courting the sun were owning it,
            as if reaching for light the secret to holding it;

to hum, pump
    your weight away from the earth,
        clasp your chapped pink hands
            around the creaking metal chains, poke

at gravity, let gravity
    poke you back again;
        to turn the sky into an endless,
            unexpected game your feet

play with space,
    with galaxies curtained off
        by the blue envelope of day; to leave
            your footprint on a cloud, let a gull

bob its gawky head
    at the ark of your up and down,
        the rushing whistle of your flight;
            to go and go, not to slow for the sake

of a jacket zipper or a bell,
    to watch the moon slowly
        become the moon, know by heart its glowing
            routine, the way it circles the earth like earth

circles the sun,
    the way it spins and spins
        and never sleeps, the way
            your legs push and pull, repeat their kick

and bend, send you
    through the cool, night-washed air
        past the angled roofs and halfway to the stars,
            then halfway to the stars again.

for Andrea

WORD

Orchard

Take the word *orchard*.
If you speak it and speak it
and speak it again, the lush
landscape of sound
will present itself
a world: *or*, an apple
fruiting on your tongue.
The hollow of this vowel:
where trees are born. Air
fills it thick as light. *ch*,
the drone of awakening bees.
They rise from the hive
you construct with your teeth,
bombard the black eyes
of the sun-petalled blooms.
ard, the bend of the low
stubborn trunks slow-wrestling
the weight of the unplucked
crop. Listen to your mouth
carving out the gnarled *r*,
muffled groan of perseverance
from the underworld of roots.
Then rest in the shadow
of the unpretentious *d*,
grassy edge of language
where imagination sleeps.

In Gratitude (II)

For the hyphen,
        yoke that binds
                two words like a bridge

spanning
        a stone-banked river,
                allying one tall-mountain-

kingdom with another;
        sinew splicing muscle
                and bone, hitching fascicle

to sheath
        in the inner-web of ankle,
                hip, wrist, hand—

coordinating
        a step, choreographing a life;
                a conductor's baton

across which rides
        the orchestra's water-bright sound
                and the very idea of tone—notation

on the staff, vibration
        on the string; lightning rod
                connecting roof to sky,

primordial dare
>to the parable of the universe
>>to bridge its own gap

like a single stroke of ink
>marrying words such as *light*
>>and *year, snow* and *capped,*

forget with *me* and *not;* thread
>that sews one flowing garment of sound
>>onto another

until each is unknowingly
>wearing the music of the other, ensemble
>>of two that moves

as one, tangos
>through a cartography of streets and news
>>and days

as across the sheen
>of a hardwood floor; at the edge of the field,
>>the gentle reach of a leaning oak

pledging fidelity
>to the cat-tailed pond
>>in a posture that has taken years to form,

the gesture
>of a thousand snow-washed moons;
>>a troth, a contract, a covenant vow

by which are fastened
>the private machineries
>>of two ready hearts—cadenced, metered,

primed—
keeping each other in tune, holding
each other in time.

for Colin and Lindsey

Retreat

The Old Hotel, Lincoln, Vermont

White-washed floorboards slant and creak.
Glass doorknobs grate when turned—
most don't turn. Women dressed

the dead in these rooms, pressed
and fixed stiff shirts and collars,
cool breezes spilling off the mountain,

churning chintz and linen curtains.
The tin roof bleeds with rust—
part of the charm for young brides,

who adjust their veils before the oak-
framed mirror in the pantry, pose
for photographs beside mournful

garden statuary. We take refuge
in paint-chipped porch-wicker, nurse
pot-bellied coffee mugs and suffer

the rooster's stubborn crow. Words
are what we are after: when we find them,
we will pin them to the unfinished arcs

of ideas. For their sake we hold
communion with laptops, gaze
at the horseless pasture, the milkweed,

and wait, or cross the street to inspect
the rusting iron mill wheel, probe
the bee-jammed mouths of honeysuckle,

cede our shivering bodies to the jade-
green hole in the river. At the campfire,
smoke annexes my nostrils. It is

the essence of all things real: winter,
car trouble, the loneliness of grief.
The damp logs whistle and hiss

like a hawk; they riddle the night
with batteries of sparks, illuminate
the fluttering underleaves of the oak,

interrupt the star-washed parable
of the sky in their ancient, garish
argument with the dark.

Possession

To have, as in to hold:

to hollow the palm
around the smooth of a snail,
inhale the sea in a single, heady breath;
yours the ships, the whales, the dangling kingdoms
of kelp, pockets full of bottle glass and scallop shells;
to tramp the burning sand, rewrite the beach
in a signature of toes, each footprint
a conquest: hard evidence of tenancy,
deliberate marking of history.

To be had, as in to be born:

to be tricked into
this lung-filling world as a prize—
a his, a hers—to be held, beholden to, inhabit
the hollow of another's hand; to be claimed by someone,
to consume and be consumed by the having, the way
the sun is had by the skin, the skin by the sun,
the way breath becomes its own private
message in the breathing.

To have had, as in to be undone:

to have held too long
the weight of a gaze, brushed a butterfly
wing and stolen its flight; to be tutored by grief,
torn from the oak that cradled your youth, the myth
of marriage to the perfect, seamless life; to become what
is no longer—a gallery of years—reach for the echo
of a voice in your dreams, the musk-thick
absence of its sound
in your bones.

Ode to the Passive Voice

The rock of the subject is plunged
       into the deep pond of the sentence, fished out

by the verb, which the object keeps
       or throws back. Therein

is conceived an elongation of thought
       prized by poets, more precious

than the music of assonance,
       the rhythmic click

of alliteration. Convention
       is mocked by this reckless display of art—

shameless exaltation of the pause, deliberate
       subversion of possessor to possession.

Ambiguity is born in the folding
       and slipping of the stone

into the blue depths
       of that dark body of words;

for a moment, truth is submerged
       by the weight of its own telling,

and I am going in after it.

Infinitive

I. Aerial

To Breathe:

(v): To inhale air and expel it,

i.e., to take in what cannot be seen—wind, night,
the memory of clouds—to be alive regardless
of awareness, to engage in the systematic practice
of becoming what will soon

disappear.

II. Sidereal

To Desire:

(v): To long for,

i.e., to be well acquainted
with distance, know by heart
the reach of constellations,
the paths of light-years
passing through the corridors

of the body.

III. Pelagic

To Spread:

(v): To extend, unfold, draw out

i.e., to stand outstretched, open
as a mirror to the waves, welcome
the pounding, the infinite rolling; embrace
what cannot be embraced: the knowing,

the not knowing.

In Gratitude (III)

For the comma, the tilted
    empty cup of it, the way
        it holds and holds off, waits,

then pins down
    the waiting: crescent moon
        dangling in the rearview

like an artifact
    of the in-between, the having left
        but not yet arrived, the time

before time counts,
    before the green glow
        of the radio light—

static buzz,
    then distant jazz:
        a bass—the pluck

and drone
    of strings, the shush
        of the brush's lulling sweep,

keys leaning into chords,
    a muted sax; a pause,
        a breath,

a dotted rest,
    the space between
        truth and fact, the knowing

and the known;
    belief—a looking back
        that says there's more

to come,
    deliberate taking in of sound,
        of night—the plaintive horn,

the arc
    of the moon—then
        a deliberate moving on.

What Men Die For Lack Of

*It is difficult to get the news from poems, yet men die miser-
ably every day for lack of what is found there.*

–William Carlos Williams

Daffodils—ten-thousand at a glance.
A globed fruit, palpable and mute.
Pockets full of lichens and seeds.
Apple-bent mossed cottage trees.
Lamb-white days, a lilting house.
Winnings risked on pitch and toss.
Boatmen's songs, mechanics' songs.
Rose moles on the skin of trout.
A cherry hung with bloom, a cherry hung with snow.
The flow of Julia's silks, the liquefaction of her clothes.
An angel robed in real linen, spun on a definite loom.
Bald and wild, the O-gape of the moon.
Telephone poles holding out their arms to birds.
A hammock, a field of sunlight between two pines.
Nine bean rows and nine and fifty swans.
A leaping tongue of bloom spared by a scythe.
Magenta pokeweed sprung in a vacant lot.
The oily, rainbowed deck of a rented boat.
White chickens, a red wheelbarrow glazed with rain.
Marbles and puddles and whistling far and wee.
Truth told slant, truth that dazzles gradually.

Ministry of Snow

Listen: someone
is scissoring the clouds, snipping

the weather
into a dazzling squall of tiny white

vowels. The hills
have become an undulating clause,

contoured
by the going under of the light,

the distant *hoo*
of an owl's lonely psalm. What

you once loved
about a dress—the delicate grammar

of its swoosh—
you have come to love about the snow:

the way
the pointed ice-ferns lisp the air,

rewrite
the yard into a stark, unrippled

fiction,
the forest into a thousand intertwining

questions.
Shhh—this is the sky unknitting itself,

wrapping you
in a baptism of cold, the monologue

of the wind
publishing its feathered rhetoric

across the roll
and dip of the field, the frozen cat-

tailed marsh.
A cardinal. A buckthorn. A sentence
of red berries
interrupted. You have entered

a kingdom
of unknowing—Holy is the sound

of forgetting.

In Objection

to the exclamation point,
        garish, gratuitous, loud—
                pure

diacritical bling:
        what a sentence does when
                it falls in love

with itself like a gallant
        peering into the lake, arrested
                by the sun's flash

on pauldrons and helmet
        and sword, glory
                defeated

by its own
        prodigious weight; a way of
                crying wolf,

pulling the alarm for fun
        (simply because it's there),
                fireworks

on an ordinary,
        unremarkable night; overkill,
                which, make no mistake,

is indeed a kind of death,
	a little like eating too much;
		a fetish, an idol,

a crutch, a charm:
	refusal to trust in rhetoric's
		inherent power

to awe, to cheer,
	to goad, to slay—a most
		unfortunate lack of faith.

Grammar Lesson

No ideas but in things.

–William Carlos Williams

A rock is not a clause.
Neither is a blizzard, except
when you enter it, snow
swallowing your ankles,
invading your socks
and no telling when—
or even whether—
it will stop.

Remove yourself
from the picture, and the blizzard
becomes a phrase—all verb
and preposition: *swirling down,*
gusting under, blowing through.

Consider the white rhetoric
of the storm, an adjective: never
have the coming together
of letters better described
a landscape.

Participles are snapshots:
you click, then stick them
on the internet like artifacts
of experience: *buried*
in a drift, *stuck* behind the plow,
harvesting the wind-*driven*
ice-flakes with your tongue.

Like an astronaut testing
the surface of the moon, you
print the snow with the rubber
stamp of your boots. *There!*—
an act of interruption, each footstep
its own exclamation-marked
interjection.

Whose storm is this?
For a moment, it is *yours*.
You have angelled it,
broomed the ground with your legs
and arms in a childlike
act of insistence: *Mine*
your padded body says,
its powdered work of art,
nothing short of a possessive.

If ever there was a noun,
it's the rock in the middle
of the field. You've sat on it
for hours, that ancient granite boulder
that taught you to ponder. Now
it's a hill, a pillow, a mountain
of feathers. No—it's the glistening arc
of the back of a whale: smooth, bright
appositive in a snowy ocean
of infinitives.

Spring Forward

The crocuses have nudged themselves up
through the snow, have opened, never
      are opening,
always daring. Ephemeral prophets,

first of the sun's spring projects, purple-
throated chorus of *will-have-beens*—
      year after
year, their oracles outlast them. Cold's

empire has not yet been undone, but
the cardinals have begun to loudly declare
      its undoing,
which is as good as the thing itself, as good

as the gutters' wild running, the spilling
of rain down the tar-slick roof, the filling
      and pooling,
the annual re-schooling of earth

in the vernal properties of water. A bud
both is and is not a flower: furled flag,
      curled-up
tongue of summer, envelope of fire—

What is this world but a seed of desire
some dream-bent farmer sowed in a field
      waiting for
the end of winter, waiting to be getting on

with the business of timothy and clover?
Light sends itself, a missive from the future:
        it's shining,
a definite *shined*, a bold, unquestionable

having shone—this because of the paths
it travels, the distances it flies. The crocuses
        shiver; still
they will not be deterred from their singing,

from the sure and heady prospect of their
having sung. The notion of green has not
        yet occurred
to the ground—twig tips, bulbs, cat-tails,

bark: all stuck in a past perfect of gray—
but green *has* occurred to the sun. A kingdom
        is in
the making—and in the making has come.

In Gratitude (IV)

For *and*, for *also*:
    songbirds perched
        between the larger facts—

a pole,
    an oak, a lonely
        neon sign—the round bulb-shaped notes

of their forms
    stringing together
        the morning, the on-and-on

of the sky's self-declaring;
    cousins of *more*, of *furthermore*,
        companion to *as well*, invisible

as persistence—
    the pointless screech
        and stall of the neighbor's

rusting Jeep, the gawk
    and cry of the garbage truck
        gulls—grammar of the second chance:

the sun's
    unasked for shining,
        the river's interminable flowing,

the way day
    after day wires and cardinals
        and even the neighbor's lantern gnome

hold fast,
    dare to inhabit their shapes,
        turn time into an endless amplification

of time, an infinite
    again, a sentence so lovely,
        so perfect that it never halts, never

closes, never turns in
    on itself like a star imploding
        or a deer looking for a place to die;

instead, sings,
    becomes a song:
        word after word, note

after note
    the cardinals, the Jeep,
        the oak, the lantern gnome sound out

what they know: *yes*—
    also, again, furthermore,
        forever, world without end.

CREED

Toward A Winter Retreat Packing List

A flashlight,
a skein of yarn,
a brush—
a flashlight
because
stars shiver forth
only their own brightness,
pinning tight the dark;
a flashlight because
a page of words
in the middle of the night
illuminates the mind
like the moon's blue net
on a pasture
of snow;
a flashlight because
it all starts
with this: *God from God,
light from light*—
and on the sixth day,
that light got stuck
in Adam's cells,
began swimming in
and out of his lungs;
a flashlight—
and a skein of yarn
because fingers love
to dance and move, love
to twine wool and flax
and doubt

into symmetry
and prayer;
a skein of yarn
out of which to spin
a scarf and the very notion
of warmth;
a skein of yarn because
to work is not
to be alone, because
what *is* community
but a sequence of purls
and knits, the invisible sum
of a thousand tiny knots?
a skein of yarn—
and a brush
because night
needs sweeping
from the hair just as sleep
needs washing from the face;
a brush because
Eve's locks were her crown
and glory,
and in this life
we could all use a little more
beauty; a brush because
questions seek an answer;
wrongdoing, forgiveness;
what is the heart after all
but a tangle of love
and fear, a perfect
snarl of desire
and resistance?
A flashlight
a skein of yarn
a brush—
because the church
is a body with feet,
fingernails, and hair,

because Christ's only hands
on earth are ours, and our hold
on earth is only
to what kindles,
what joins,
      what sings,

what sifts,
           what suffers,

what renews.

Reading Hopkins at the Auto Repair

Glory be to God for oil-stained hands—
  Creased black with work, for shirts stained thick with grease
    For wrenches, chargers, filters, hoists, and jacks,
And all who wield them, use them, run them, fix
  The ills of motors, axels, starters, belts
    With method, art, dexterity, and grace.

For springs replaced, transmission fluid changed,
  Whatever coils and hoses patched or spliced
    Whatever leaks repaired (such holy work!)
He sees to bolts who also sees to souls:
          Praise Him.

Before the Shape-Note Sing

Here is where water becomes air,
the small reservoirs of our bodies exhale
streams of sound, a waterfall of drone
and shout, except this waterfall goes up—

up into the deep blue cup of the dome,
past the classical columns, the three-tiered
chandelier, crashing into the white heights
of the walls, the clear, illuminated windows.

It is hot. We will sweat. We will heel
the wooden floor, nod, raise our forearms,
shape loud notes out of the sacred wrecks
of ourselves. If ever we will speak in tongues,

it will be here, here where water
turns into air. This is a kind of work—
this is a kind of grace. A voice will rise
above the rest, a fan keep time.

A woman will close her eyes, but her mouth
will not stop. The sound is a river
she has come here to enter. Everyone around her
is singing—singing her up to the altar,

singing her into the river. When the voices
stop, she will return to the wet skin
of her neck, the tired skin of her aching feet,
shift her weight. Someone will call out a pitch,

pages turn, voices slide up and down
the scale, find their notes. Heads will dip
and nod, forearms rise. Out of the broken
harps of our bodies: a holy noise.

Canticle (II)

Sing through the lathe of your mouth.
Sing on the salt of your breath.
Sing through the rigs of your lungs.
Sing out your debts to the earth.

Sing with the throat of a hawk.
Sing in the slang of your blood.
Sing from the kiln of your hope.
Sing till the stones turn to bread.

Sing like a prophet in chains.
Sing at the crux of your fears.
Sing holy glyphs with your hands.
Sing what your tongue cannot bear.

Sing without clenching your loss.
Sing till the nebulae cease.
Sing in the tremble of grace.
Sing and do not hold your peace.

Make Me Plow Blade

Make me plow blade, implement
for the deep earth. Forge me blue
with heat, Lord of flame. Blow
strong the bellows. Let the bellows
sing; baptize me in song. Let ring

anvil, hammer, iron, tong. Away
the slag, away the dull. Draw me
sharp as the chine of a scythe,
sharp as sun glint, sharp as steel.
Lord of moldboard, coulter, land-

side, heel, temper me raw in water
and salt. Mark me with ash. Bathe
me in flux. Teach me syntax of edge
and point, syntax of furrow, syntax
of stone. Lord of harvest, fit me

to rend, fit my tongue to till. Oh be
not done till the yoke holds fast,
the share proves keen. Oh be not
done till the ground gives way, O
Shaper of earth, of blade, of song.

Genesis (III)

Psalm 139:13–16

Before light
was mine, and the air that sways the wheat fields
and clover filled

the O-sacs
of my lungs, you plucked a harvest of stars
from the universe

of my mother's
womb—those shining, singing things called
cells—sewed them

into nodes
and valves—follicles, ossicles, auricles, ducts;
hinged humerus

to radius,
stitched iris to retina, cornea to macula, then
attached the palabra;

you invented
my appendix, my gallbladder, my epiglottis,
my spleen,

all manner
of fascia and humor and gland, took pleasure
in the particular

                placement
of the atlas, the jaw-like pedestal of my cranium,
                that membraned

                chamber
of ganglia and nerve, dark factory of thought:
                and here

                is where
you signed your name, laid claim to this tight
                constellation

                of salts,
this breathing, ticking scaffold of dreams.
                Not in terms

                of lobule, lymph
ligament, or vein did you leave your mark,
                but rather, this:

                an affinity
for zinnias, for swallows and plums, and questions
                about the lives of ferns.

Offering

We are born into giving, enter the living
ark of the world through the act of breaking—

a splitting of self from self, which is itself
an act of becoming. We are what—and because—

we have been given, defined by our taking,
our necessary depending; our very breathing,

hard evidence of the offering. Loving
is a kind of dying, a turning in (or over)

of the self in an act of yielding, the heart
becoming what it is in the sharp moments

of breaking, then the long, drawn-out winter
of its complicated re-making. Ubiquitous

the ceding: ancient oaks bequeathing tall,
knotted bodies to the earth, winged insects

their short, sunlit minutes to the air; a vast,
perpetual sacrifice is the ocean on the altar

of the shell-glittering shore. This morning
the sun bestows itself in a glorious unfolding;

light re-invents the day—day makes itself
out of night, quarrels with, then surrenders

to the dark, is what it is because it continually
gives itself over to that which it is not.

Psalm

Praise to the Weaver of symmetries,
Sustainer of stars and all harmonies,
Inventor of light and its subtleties,
Designer of souls and anatomies.

Praise to the Weigher of gravities,
Author of oceans and mysteries,
Director of blood's circularities,
Adjuster of winds and proximities.

Praise to the Sculptor of galaxies,
Prober of hearts and all certainties,
Tuner of cells and their frequencies,
Conductor of night's musicalities.

Praise to the Wounder of enmities,
Mender of losses and maladies,
Defeater of earthly hostilities,
Repairer of torn mutualities.

Praise to the Coiner of poetries,
Lover of love and its currencies,
Confounder of death and its secrecies,
Redeemer of dust and infinities.

How to Prepare for the Second Coming

Start by recalling the absolute goodness of rain
and repent for every grumble you have ever made
about the weather (this will take approximately

forever.) Next, you will want to commit a theft:
with deft lock-picking and a shrewd hand, steal
back the hours you fed to the hungry god of work,

then squander them on hydrangeas, Wordsworth,
voluntary sidewalk repair. Teach a child to lace
a shoe (your child or another's—any four-year-old

will do), and while you're at it, set the alarm
for three, and fumble through the dark to the pond
to guard the salamanders as they cross the road. If,

having accomplished these tasks, you wish
to go on, sit at your desk and carefully design
a few radical acts of grace, by which I mean

murder (of a sort): you must willfully, passionately
kill the living, breathing debt owed you by those
who stole your goods, your rights, or the jewel

that was the beating muscle of your hope. Apart
from this, you cannot know the full extent of love.
(For precedent, refer to the cross). Thrust

your nails into dirt and plant a few seeds (carrots,
radishes, chives); indeed, get scandalously intimate
with the earth. After all, it is where you will live

when the lamb lies down with the lion, and the lion
has become your friend. And when the water
of the new world breaks, all is said and done (heaven

and earth made one as the prophets foretold),
you will lose each doubt to a song—which is
a kind of praise—and reap the good you sowed.

Inheritance

In the end, the light will be yours—
        you will wear it like a song. No longer

will the small instrument of your heart
        click its private music in the dark;

each note will explode into white,
        wind-swirled blossoms of desire. You will enter

a vast country unbounded by words,
        the kind you have visited in dreams.

Here, air and light are the language
        you speak. When you arrive, you will be known

the way, since you were a child, the moss
        at the water's edge has honored the curved press

of your feet, measured the weight of your days;
        the oak at the bend in the brook,

the slow-moving river of your years.
        All your tears have prepared you for this:

a *now* that has ousted *after* and *if*
        and *then*, a geography unhindered by time,

a new kind of green, an unforeseen fellowship
        with the finches, the pines, an entering

into their song, a longing so full,
        so intricate and free it has become

the continent in which you live. You will forgive
        the dark, understand that every work of art

has been a map, every summer dusk a call,
        milkweed soft and hardly there. Now

you can hear what never could be heard
        before: day opening up into day, the blue

pool of the sky brimming over like a promise,
        wind covenanting with the clouds,

courting the yellow-feathered birds.
        Your hands will shape objects out of ideas,

your feet not just walk, but walk toward,
        devoting themselves over and over again

to the earth, larkspur lilting like psalms
        across your path. At once, you will stop,

ponder the wonder of the tongue, the willing hum
        of bees, how they zip and hover and never

sleep—how one day, unknowing, you were born,
        became who you are—a breath, a stem, a leaf

in the wind—how the wind gifted you
        with shape, whittled you into the image

of your name—how your name became
        a wild and shimmering field of asters: day

after day, you have wandered its tousled edges,
        listened to the distant grasses list and bow

their foreign praises. Morning gives way
        to evening, evening to morning—your fingers

spin offerings of prose out of that endless, star-pierced
        turning. This, the constellations

have taught you: the heart was made for light—
        you have seen it in the silver flash

of a fish, the shiver of a dancer's rippled sash;
        you have touched it—the hem of the sun—

and lived, and ever since, your breathing
        has been a gentle waiting, a pilgrim's

slow and barefoot journeying. Radiance
        is filling the temple of your bones, fitting you

for the bright orchard of its kingdom; branches
        are bending themselves into a dwelling.

Prayer

Be map, be lamp, be flame
for my way, be sole of my
shoe, be stride of my walk,

be mountain, be forest, be
cool of the shade, be wind
in the pine, be silence of

deer, be bridge, be stream,
be bend in the trail, be the
slope of my climb, be the

grip of my tread, be my rise
when I fall, be my rest when
I sit, be the stone in my boot,

be my will to forgive, yes
be compass, be owl song,
be north, be my end, my be-

ginning, my wandering, my
weeping, my word, oh be
blanket of sky, oh be fruit

on my tongue, oh be lark-
spur, be raindrop, be stars
holding fast, be the first

glint of dawn, be the dew on
the grass, be my waking, my
prize, my horizon, my path.

for Kevin and Rebecca

Benediction

May you hold
the candle of our coming together
in the tabernacle

of your heart
like a small treasure of fire.
May its light

live in you
like music. Work that is good,
may it borrow

your hands—
Sweet be the fruit of your labors.
Let your making

and your doing
twin the beauty of your being.
May you become

your calling,
even as for a moment here
you have become

an offering.
Words that nourish bones
be yours,

yours, a love
that shelters and holds. Go—
        gift the bread

        of friendship,
spill the wine of sacrifice. Evening
        approaches;

        the table
is set. There are many ways
        to wash feet.

Creed

I believe in the life of the word,
the diplomacy of food. I believe in salt-thick,
ancient seas and the absoluteness of blue.
A poem is an ark, a suitcase in which to pack
the universe—I believe in the universality
of art, of human thirst

for a place. I believe in Adam's work
of naming breath and weather—all manner
of wind and stillness, humidity
and heat. I believe in the audacity
of light, the patience of cedars,
the innocence of weeds. I believe

in apologies, soliloquies, speaking
in tongues; the underwater
operas of whales, the secret
prayer rituals of bees. As for miracles—
the perfection of cells, the integrity
of wings—I believe. Bones

know the dust from which they come;
all music spins through space on just
a breath. I believe in that grand economy
of love that counts the tiny death
of every fern and white-tailed fox.
I believe in the healing ministry

of phlox, the holy brokenness of saints,
the fortuity of faults—of making
and then redeeming mistakes. Who dares
brush off the auguries of a storm, disdain
the lilting eulogies of the moon? To dance
is nothing less than an act of faith

in what the prophets sang. I believe
in the genius of children and the goodness
of sleep, the eternal impulse to create. For love
of God and the human race, I believe
in the elegance of insects, the imminence
of winter, the free enterprise of grace.

Acknowledgements

Appreciation is extended to the editors of these journals and magazines, where the following poems first appeared:

Altarwork: "Prayer," "Learning How to Pray," "Canticle (II)"
The Anglican Theological Review: "Before the Shape-Note Sing"
Ascent: "Ministry of Snow"
The Christian Century: "Make Me Plow Blade"
Crab Orchard Review: "The Glassed World"
Dappled Things: "Genesis (I)" "Hallowed Be," "Reading Hopkins at the Auto Repair"
Flycatcher: "Matins"
Glass: "The Way a Fish"
Grey Sparrow Review: "Infinitive," "Vespers"
Midwest Quarterly: "Genesis (II)"
Plough.com: "Make Me Red-tailed Hawk," "Make Me Sheet Moss"
River Oak Review: "Orchard"
Ruminate: "Genesis (III)"
Spiritus: "In Gratitude (for *and* and *also*)"
Terrain: "Heron," "Thalassic"
Windhover: "Benediction"

"Creed," "How To Prepare for the Second Coming," and "Spring Forward" appear in *Between Midnight and Dawn: A Literary Guide to Prayer for Lent, Holy Week, and Eastertide* edited by Sarah Arthur (Paraclete Press).

"Canticle (I)" was commissioned by the Vermont Choral Union directed by Jeff Rehbach, and set to music by Christina Whitten Thomas as part of the song cycle "Songs of Gold."

COLLECTIONS IN THIS SERIES INCLUDE:

Six Sundays toward a Seventh by Sydney Lea

Epitaphs for the Journey by Paul Mariani

Within This Tree of Bones by Robert Siegel

Particular Scandals by Julie L. Moore

Gold by Barbara Crooker

A Word In My Mouth by Robert Cording

Say This Prayer into the Past by Paul J. Willis

Scape by Luci Shaw

Conspiracy of Light by D. S. Martin

Second Sky by Tania Runyan

Remembering Jesus by John Leax

What Cannot Be Fixed by Jill Peláez Baumgaertner

Still Working It Out by Brad Davis

The Hatching of the Heart by Margo Swiss

Collage of Seoul by Jae Newman

Twisted Shapes of Light by William Jolliff

These Intricacies by Dave Harrity

Where the Sky Opens by Laurie Klein

True, False, None of the Above by Marjorie Maddox

The Turning Aside anthology edited by D.S. Martin

Falter by Marjorie Stelmach

Phases by Mischa Willett

Second Bloom by Anya Krugovoy Silver

Adam, Eve, & the Riders of the Apocalypse
anthology edited by D.S. Martin

Your Twenty-First Century Prayer Life by Nathaniel Lee Hansen

Made in United States
Orlando, FL
14 May 2024

46847651R00082